Published by Creative Education
P.O. Box 227
Mankato, Minnesota 56002
Creative Education is an imprint of The Creative Company

Design by Stephanie Blumenthal; Production by Heidi Thompson

Photographs by Getty Images (De Agostini, Hulton Archive, Hulton
Archive/Stringer, Photopix, Roger Viollet Collection, Travelpix Ltd,
Oliver Benn, Terry Donnelly, Robert Francis, Heinrich Hansen,
Marie Hickman, Hideo Kurihara, Joseph Nash,
James Stephanoff, Dallas Stribley, Adina Tovy, Charlie Waite)
Corbis (Roy Rainford/Robert Harding World Imagery)

Library of Congress Cataloging-in-Publication Data

Bodden, Valerie.
Castles / by Valerie Bodden.
p. cm. — (Built to last)
Includes index.
ISBN 978-1-58341-561-0
1. Castles—Juvenile literature.
2. Civilization, Medieval—Juvenile literature. I. Title. II. Series.

GT3550.B64 2007
728.8'10902—dc22   2006101006

First edition
2 4 6 8 9 7 5 3 1

CASTLES | VALERIE BODDEN

CREATIVE ✦ EDUCATION

A huge castle stands on top of a high hill. Tall towers reach up toward the sky. The castle looks very pretty. But it was not built just to be pretty. It was built to keep people safe.

Windsor Castle is 900 years old

ONE CASTLE THAT IS STILL LIVED IN TODAY IS WINDSOR CASTLE. WINDSOR CASTLE IS IN ENGLAND. THE QUEEN OF ENGLAND LIVES IN IT.

SOMETIMES A LORD WANTED TO BUILD HIS CASTLE WHERE THERE WAS NO HILL. IN THAT CASE, HE MIGHT DECIDE TO MAKE HIS OWN HILL!

Castles were built in high places

Most castles were built in Europe (*YOOR-up*). They were built in medieval (*mih-DEE-vul*) times. There were lots of wars during these times. People tried to take each other's lands and homes. Rich men decided to make strong buildings that would be hard to attack. They built castles.

Many castles were built on top of hills.
This way, people could see their enemies
coming from far off. Most castles had
walls around them. Some castles had tall
towers. Soldiers could shoot arrows from
the top of the walls and towers.

Some castles were surrounded by a
deep ditch. The ditch was called a
moat. There was water in the moat.
This made it hard for enemies to get
close to the castle.

Stone castles last a long time

MOST CASTLES WERE BUILT OUT OF STONE. THIS WAY, ENEMIES COULD NOT BURN THEM DOWN.

Most castles had a drawbridge over the moat. A drawbridge is a bridge that can be raised up so that no one can cross it.

Moats went all around castles

Inside, most castles had a big room called the Great Hall. People ate in the Great Hall. They listened to music there. Some people slept in the Great Hall. Castles had bedrooms, too. The best bedroom was for the castle's lord.

KNIGHTS WERE FIGHTERS
WHO WORKED FOR A KING
OR LORD. MANY KNIGHTS
LIVED IN CASTLES OR HAD
THEIR OWN CASTLES.

Knights helped keep castles safe

There were other buildings inside of a castle's walls, too. There was a kitchen. There were barns. Most castles had a small church.

Some castles had big kitchens

Lots of people lived in a castle. The lord and his wife lived there. So did the people who worked for them. More than 100 people lived in some castles!

Fires gave castles a smoky smell

IN THE FIRST CASTLES, AN OPEN FIRE PIT WAS USED TO HEAT THE GREAT HALL. THIS MADE THE ROOM SMOKY.

Today, most castles are not lived in. Some have been made into hotels. Others are now **museums** (*myoo-ZEE-umz*). People can walk through them and imagine what it was like to live in them!

Castle dungeons were like jails

MANY CASTLES HAD DUNGEONS (*DUN-junz*). THESE WERE COLD, **DAMP** UNDERGROUND ROOMS WHERE PRISONERS WERE KEPT.